FAREWELLIA
a la Aralee

*his suite of poems after her,
delivered at the Aralee Strange Tribute,
Northside Tavern, Cincinnati, 15 Sept 2013…*

by
Ralph La Charity

DOS MADRES
2014

DOS MADRES PRESS INC.
P.O. Box 294, Loveland, Ohio 45140
www.dosmadres.com   editor@dosmadres.com

Dos Madres is dedicated to the belief that the small press is essential to the vitality of contemporary literature as a carrier of the new voice, as well as the older, sometimes forgotten voices of the past. And in an ever more virtual world, to the creation of fine books pleasing to the eye and hand.

Dos Madres is named in honor of Vera Murphy and Libbie Hughes, the "Dos Madres" whose contributions have made this press possible.

Dos Madres Press, Inc. is an Ohio Not For Profit Corporation and a 501 (c) (3) qualified public charity. Contributions are tax deductible.

Executive Editor: Robert J. Murphy

Illustration & Book Design: Elizabeth H. Murphy
www.illusionstudios.net

Typset in Adobe Garamond Pro & Cochin
ISBN 978-1-939929-10-5
Library of Congress Control Number: 2014932330

Acknowledgements
Author photo / Ralph La Charity, Cincinnati
Aralee's headshot / Dawn Richards, Scioto County, Ohio
Cover photo / Elizabeth Logan Harris, Brooklyn NY
Vocal CD master / engineered by Randal C. Campbell
of Sonic Arts of Cincinnati

First Edition

Copyright 2014 Dos Madres Press inc.
All rights to reproduction of the text, quotation,
and translation reside with the author.

POEM TITLES:

Man in Hat

what we'll be do

the Old Ones

Sleight of Disappear

Dark Lawful Rhythmic Infinity

VICTOR WEAVE

Aralee Felt Strange

Dancin' in the Wake

Song of Mourning and Celebration

APPENDIX:

CINEMANUENSING
(a writ of *habeus corpus poetique*)
1998
facsimile edition

MAN IN HAT

we knew

what was coming
so did she

fat train bearing down
and no de-rail in sight

shook the ground
for miles around

shook the thistles
and the briars

shook the willows, too

man in gaudy hat
sat at rail's end

met that fat
head on

ɸ

WHAT WE'LL BE DO

caught our breath in tears where they ran

   the whole of crossing over's
       the whole of what we do here

stutter-trills & hop-slides fare thee well
the echo's cadence till namore remains the same

the whole of what we do here won't be done again
makes you wonder why we remember what we do

staying put's not what we'll be do
       nay, tis not what we'll achieve

I walked off with things in hand I couldn't drop
I knew I'd bring it back but maybe not

the urge to stop still waits upon the rise

crossings bear namore the tilting shade
these shadows stride askance & dip askew

reverberate head bones these tones we do
each line of every song escapes in vain

all rhythms host all breath & hearts the same

    the whole of what we're doing's all
   the whole of crossing over

tis the patch of light briefly where we stood
tis the is of this that winks away

⚘

THE OLD ONES

do the old ones who are gone
hear us when we ring in, singing ?
I believe they do. It is all & precisely
what they must do. When I'm gone
I'll listen, too . . .

the old ones who are still here
have vivid dreams of those they knew
who now inhabit silence --- O !
overpopulated ear, cocked
& rotting & never not filled with
such Promise . . .

since what the dead do is listen it is
crucial never to address them.
Every uttered word is already overheard
& their overwhelming Promise, as
last mute magicians cocked & rotting
is that the word Alive go
elsewhere always, antic

                      & Aloud . . .

           ⳨ ⳨

SLEIGHT OF DISAPPEAR

in magic illusion decrees not what's here be there
nor that halved be wholed or that sink up-float no
no no as margareta Queen of Denial'd always say

that Aralee was still here her still heart-Felt declared
too frail to hold dispute with or weep wide-eyed oh!
how the already gone-on guffaw down raw oysters!
(ever eat raw oysters with Aralee ? we did… we did)

gal was a smoker's all I know don't y'know's why
Izzy went off walking with Linda at Grady's that day
Ben stood still in the rain so long down by the riverside

tonight we danced in the wake an eight hours drive away
a whole week & one day later slow dancing till admitted :
I injure easy but recover quick's how it got put out not

that that's a lie but neither was our Dance & you were
taller & heavier & the Dance ended over easy all alone

DARK LAWFUL RHYTHMIC INFINITY
BENEATH EACH US & ALL

there is a city beneath CinCinity
an Infinity nightly infinitely Intimate
Infinite definite Nights of CinCinity
an Infinity infinitely That

infinitely City beneath CinCinity
intimately Infinite yet Definite
& nightly undefined & indefinable
yet definitely Under CinCinity
despite each Intimacy & Every infinity

a definitively undefined CinCinity suborned
a City that just sits there, unplumbed
indefinably unplumbable but utterly There
Citying darkly underfoot & wide-eyed

a City within & below gazing back up
an Infinity internal eternally watchful
an absolute Other absolutely There
where Here waits knowing More as Law

where CinCinity idles busy As law
& Infinity is infinitely Idle
& Law idles intimately & not at All untimidly
& CinCinity looks definitely the other way
the Other Way over-mining
the Other CinCinity

beneath each Us   & All

ɸ

VICTOR WEAVE

Call the hearth at home friendly fire
Call the cold hours' starlight friendly fire
& while friendly fire's everywhere & forever
this fire reaps & preys
this fire lights both ways

Mine eyes flake with unexploded impact

Mine eyes infiltrate jellied tank towns
power walking well-heeled graft
along sweat-banded loopy beachheads

Call the pain of birth friendly fire
Call the cries of babes friendly fire
& while friendly fire's everywhere & forever
this fire gives & takes away
this fire leaps & falls both ways

Mine eyes belly up to the guile larder
guild guilt & fool around

Mine eyes climb hand over hand
collateral pig's foot caked
camel spit in the pentagon pool

    Call the threaded looms friendly fire
    Call our darkened room friendly fire
& while friendly fire's everywhere & forever
        this fire flays & it slays
        this fire weaves both ways

            Mine eyes elope with pack rats
            reckless shuttlecocks are mine eyes

            Mine eyes field strip jackets whisker-coned
            ambulatory un-deloused starvation buffer
            bubs of trench flag bridges downed

    Call lakes when they shine friendly fire
    Call waves when they break friendly fire
& while friendly fire's everywhere & forever
        this fire aches & it craves
        this fire bathes both ways

            Mine eyes have seen shroudy captives file
            down choked dune-tides that bind

            Mine eyes align beloved warps click-beetled
            below bellowing hypno-stipulative pushovers
            registrating duality-crest bledfellows

Call grasses when they sway friendly fire
Call fireflies in their dance friendly fire
& while friendly fire's everywhere & forever
    this fire burns where it braves
      this fire churns both ways

          Mine eyes are incandescent lusty fleas
          procreant witnesses swallowed by the sword

          Mine eyes crosshair whole quilts of plague ghetto
          ethers inhaled   stuttering grease clams
          global intake cringe-roots, boot-lamped

Call the morning star friendly fire
Call the setting sun friendly fire
& while friendly fire's everywhere & forever
    this fire eats the days
    this fire bites both ways

          Mine eyes muster the tar pits' babble
          they savor lies seasoned & enshrined

          Mine eyes hourglass nay-knowing cloverleafs
          new-mown chopped quicksaw sanddust mounds
          of crater-sculpt horizon ramps, offed

Call the comet's tail friendly fire
Call the new moon's silver friendly fire
& while friendly fire's everywhere & forever
this fire sleeps within the blaze
this fire wakes both ways

  Mine eyes cook dawn's early light
  & the smoke of twilight's fast breathing

  Mine eyes lock headlong baggy & bodiless
  consensus-swept support nodes
  giddy on dire World Cop Love

  Mine eyes whorl whorish ado & anon

ϕ

ARALEE FELT STRANGE 1943 – 2013

You got to walk this lonesome valley
You got to walk it by Yourself

She was a Felt, our Felt

"not that they have what we don't have,
But that we can be close to them and they
will expand into what it is we lack… they fill
a place in us we didn't even know we didn't have… "

    Oh
nobody else can walk it for you
you got to walk it by Yourself

She was a Felt indeed

"not a Thought, not a person
who touches us via our minds
so much as via our souls even
more than our hearts, Ay…
She was a Felt."

& she loved her felt peeps
& we were All her felt peeps

*"Felts have many many lovers,
and Felts are all so frequently
all alone…"*

y'all're them & know
y'all're them without
a shadow of a doubt

*"she knew how to share –
I suppose it was another
of her teachings, right
up there with
how to mourn…"*

& us in her wake are
her felt-Dwellers
      Felt-dwellers all

*"not so many Felts around, y'know…
kind of a rare breed, akin to rara avis, eh?"*

o my Love
my true Love
I hunger
for Your

that you are loved despite
this the Known, shared

"we are attracted to the Felts
in our lives because of certain
talents we do not have… Felts are
squarely in our blind spots, big as life… "

that You were Felt & known
we Felt-dwellers knew You
knew & Know & felt
Your very Felt indeed

DANCIN' IN THE WAKE

yea, sun's
goin' down, Aralee

let's go swimmin'

light as ash you are
girlfriend, let's go
dancin' in yonder spring

nay, girl, lemme
dance your ash in
that River, you do
know the One…

bitter clear River
River Rive & begone
River Dove & begot
River of Many Returns

of Birmingham
& Manhattan, too

River o' Grief & no relief
River Flow & River Swing

floodtide weep Rejoice !
floodtide woe Bedamned !

you know the One
we'll be back in twenty
maybe half again
we'll be back, girlfriend

dancers swim
the floodtide vale
Dancers !

swim the blooded veil
see thru every wave
sing & sear, my love
sing & seer, o Poet

those wavelets
o how they suck & lap
ankle drag slap & chill

bullfrog burp
to beat the band
Benny the Hat bird-rapt
down beneath those
weep-dript boughs
sax tones bend
& laughter, too
toothsome you
skip to m'lou
toot sweet, too

o we're dancin'
White Girl
dancin'
      down the Flow

yea we're dancin'
White Girl
dancin'
      down the Flow !

⚘

SONG OF MOURNING AND CELEBRATION

on the I-Can Sea where

the Moon says I Love You

on the I-Can Sea where the Moon

says I Love You

Red Sky falling on the I-Can Sea sing

Sun will Dawn   Sun will Dawn

We are falling to sleep
& the shade is stealing upon us

Briefly, we awaken
move in Light lightly
glancing bravely at all we can see

Others move in, the others
mine our courage with their moving
as we mine theirs with ours
so it goes, miners all, glancing bravely

that ol' Acoustic Sun

    that ol' Acoustic Sun

        that ol' Acoustic sun's

            all wet

sun sounds bright today

sun pounds out every beat

sun shines & downs

    & yawns & calls

    can't Be no other Way

Our sleep has been & will be long
the theft total when it comes

Slowly, our eyes focus
the subtle colors of the field
how the lover's face dims & brightens

We choose from what comes closest
& what comes closest chooses from us
& we are not afraid so much as
quickened by the shade

on the I-Can Sea where

    the Waves say I Love You

on the I-Can Sea where the Waves

    say I Love You

Red Sky sailing on the I-Can Sea sing

    Sun will Dawn   Sun will Dawn

As whitecaps to the moon & blades to the breeze
as poppies to the distant & dominant sun

Quickly now! So much being irresistible
so tiny & so utterly grand
we've hardly time to tell, yet we know

comes a murmur & a stirring
the knowing ground slopes towards us
the kiss of light widens & grows deep
Now the embrace, Now the cause of ALL

that ol' Acoustic Sun

    that ol' Acoustic Sun

        that ol' Acoustic sun's

            all wet

and if everyone's a God

and Light is everywhere

tell me, How you gonna Shine

How you gonna Shine

        Acoustic Sun ?

Exquisite colors and calls no man can still
the whole a gift from the Beginning

Now for you both, each other
While one rests the other watches
Your glancings newly
        served as brave regard

Now for you a moving within
each other along the now-lit slope
& so you go, each Light to the other
& so you go, each shelter to the Shade

on the I-Can Sea where

a Rose says I Love You

on the I-Can Sea where the Rose

says I Love You

Red Sky rising on the I-Can Sea sing

Sun will Dawn   Sun will Dawn

APPENDIX:

CINEMANUENSING
(a writ of *habeus corpus poetique*)
1998

facsimile edition

ra's elf the younger's
CINEMANUENSING
(a writ of *habeus corpus poetique*)

aloud allowed imPress
CINCINNATI '98

o! *thespi-skalds* . . .

" why sharks're
        the evaporate collaborative

        seizures of leakage
        admitted on the cusp
of myriad quick cutting

        willful rogue drollery
      which sway balances
as tidal flux frisked

unsung begot everly lasted

      flimflamfilmy fingered
a long way from any coast

      looking without blink "

*

(briefs for Aralee & the Poets Chorus . . .

the poems:

SHARK DRAG
SPLASH RESEARCH
STAMPEDIMENTA
DOLLY PARTING
LIQUIDITY LAGER
PURCHASE GUARANTEED
THE VISIONAL, *EN PASSANT*

the prose:

ART PEPPER FALLS O'ER OHIO
SASHA ENTRAINS THE TAO OF GETHSEMANI
A LIFTING BEFALLETH MAIN STREET
IN THE THEATRE OF PERFECT SPEED
LISTENING POST TEMPO BREATH
THINGS A BODY TO ITS DETRIMENT GETS USED TO
SPECIFICA *y* CONCLUSIVITAS

copywright 1998: for poet/collagist/cinemanuensis, Ralph La Charity

Art Pepper Falls O'er Ohio . . .

Most of what was called landscape had yet to break the surface of consciousness in the form of record, whether that record be in the manner of word, drawing, painting, photograph, or even cinematograph (so it is that having reached legal drinking age actually qualifies any random citizen as having walked in the flesh thru limitlessly greater pan-actuality than ever has been recorded thru all of history

                or so it is stated

herewith & for the purpose of argument: King James & all his elegantly starved scribes never saw nuthin' yet, which is why it is so much a fated lure to mock and mime them, which we the Poets do, incessantly & evermore, lest we stand revealed as mere cultists, reaping even as we rave, howsoever sly withal

                for also it is maintained forthwith

that all we stand and ride upon throughout the Midwest is but flood time or ice ages brooded on since before history; that to lift upward thru this immemorial brooding is unfathomably & without redemption curséd from *every* angle; that to trespass upon the incomplete record with new everDance of any kind is simply the only worthwhile endeavor the spirit might cause itself to wreak in this entire region; finally, that Art Pepper's recording of Landscape will be our guidon where we wend . . .

Sasha Entrains the Tao of Gethsemani . . .

Other than to say it does mean something, it is hard to say what exactly it does mean that engine one-five-two breathes within hearing distance of the monastery at Gethsemani in central Kentucky, west of Lexington, south of Louisville; that yes, flattened pennies can be found on the track at New Haven, Kentucky, that engine's home station; and that the rhythm of locomotive one-five-two when it heats in the yard outside its barn is percussively a wonder, as if that engine were a band, its own band, valving steam through timed iron cycles quite the same as if everyone who came within earshot could be counted on to dance everly lasted, through sunshine, rain, fog, and tornado-twist, aye, dance and grin upon the instant, as if the instant had not occured at the beginning of this century rather than now, at its end.
Or the bridge to Southgate House, the one that puts you at the base of York Street. Take the first alley to the left, don't park on the left side ($10 ticket, band or no). Or turn left at the intersection where Cunningham's York St Cafe is, then left again onto Monmouth till you find the two Brass bars, Bull and Ass. Ass will play your cassette if you arrive around 7:30 and the barmaid likes you. The sound system at the Brass Ass is a locomotive rounding a bend pushing fifty, but it's the sound system at the York that has seduced the poets. The York sound has intimate power, like singing in the shower. At the Ass, it helps if you can drive pile, or, at the very least slay a lot of tail. Until recently, you brought your own sound to the Southgate, but Ross fixed that, and now it's up to Scott to keep the feedback off Parker... yea, William and his dance partner Patricia follow the tao to Atlanta come dawn.

The tao is how Sasha got himself out of bed today, him, having samba'd Friday night away at Yukio's joint before shutting down Kaldi's amidst the tumult on Main Steet. The tumult on Main Street's getting a new addition come Sunday when Aralee's filming of her *THIS TRAIN* ratchets into Kaldi's. She used to live on Main up around 14th for years before heading off to Peach Mountain, four counties over. Some say she got hit by lightning up there on the Peach, and that that's why she's had a bolt tattoo'd to the side of her face, and that that's why Michael, her film's po'-nomad anrog/protag, nods off so: Michael's a lightning strike survivor. As for the tao, there was an introductory talk on the tao at the Acquarius at one today, early for ol' Sash. And he tells me he hates the damn film 'cause he loves his coffee and the filming's locating over at Kaldi's for the whole week upcoming. As for the tao, don't let your coffee jones dire down the flow around you and within you, beyond you and beneath you... in the landscape of the city, King James' mountain gets rounded by a train of many colors, rhythming & boiling & clacking, a train of many sexes, yearning & recoiling & returning to the fray, a train wedding the Valley of the Ohio in August with the cells of San Quentin in Marin County in September with arpeggios along the Maumee near Michigan come October. And who's to say whether or not Jay's bomba-bumptious dirge music better captures the urge to bring Peach Mountain to bear along Main Street than does any other dirge music, for it is difficult to improvise a blues when nothing's happening save the desire to save the monks and the topless dancers of Newport from November's chores of pick, choose, & cut.

A Lifting Befalleth Main Street . . .

Come summer in Cincinnati, with the memory of all those trees upcountry and this Midwestern sea a tide both transpontane & tsunami-torpid on the juice of appetite, the mountain nods with deadpan longing, a swell and a heave cowed and drowsy, much a dumbstruck immensity viewed from afar, its hollers & nooks, its crannies & runs, stained with grief & the forgetting that is every manner of drain & drag upon the spirit of making. Would we kiss in the neglected doorway, our headsets all tuned in, our lunch across the way noodly & lettuced & free. Would that lace & boots, dashikis & togobrellas, noserings & flatpenny pendants & silverish trainboxes, mark our mockery of said impotence.

We some of us miss the music sorely. Miss improv & spontane. We want the sound of surprise as an actual *being*. We stand isolate & appalled at actual poets pretending to be themselves. Appalled at Kaldi's creaky floorboards & wheezy coolers, we wonder at the New Yorkers amongst us, those pros. We watch Jane's ribcage & wonder how those ribs could semi-attract... we're afraid for the glassy-eyed caterer who is unable to admit his out of synchedness at such an hour.

Tis the wee hours as the citizens of this neighborhood mutely glower past our purpose. Years of poetblood stain Kaldi's creak. Poets've died here. Their spirits swim in the night air. Poets have died everywhere, nor is much that swims in the torpidity benign. Cincinnati ain't paying for none of this. Whoever's getting paid ain't getting paid enough. Much that swims August currents is overdue & terribly resentful, but these New Yorkers miss their own city & they miss the sharks that never nod nor drowse nor do they fake applause or even applaud anything at all. Towers & stadia nurse predators on the prowl. There are forces and those forces feed the hour by tolling dumbly. The United Fruit Company dolls itself up as a banana Miranda. Soapsuds & diarrhea grease Carmen's hoary dance down the alleyways. Tierney would have made the most splendid Ophelia, don't y'think? We need Joe to open up the 1207 this night, we need an actual opening in the seams of Aralee's intricate homecoming hullabaloo, we need Terri to flash the hour, Kenny to horn in, Matt to pogo, Anne to saxophonicize, Mickey to Morgan eerily in a whited robe, Larry to hambonicize Stevie's headshakery, we want some thunderfarts, some Bronx cheers, catcalls & hecklery... we get tedium & layers of complexity & a hungry heart that has prepared itself for this moment for years: We get Aralee.

The ladies are having a grand, grand time. Aralee doesn't want to hear about swimming with sharks, she is adamant about that not being what's at all a part of this. There is a purity that stares willfully through predatory deadpans & she claims that purity. No one will deny her. No sharkish nays will long obtrude.

You can walk from here through downtown and cross the bridge to old Kentucky, of which Bill Polak has sung. Across the river to the titty bars that don't do live music either. That the river flows submerged beneath the sea of August, & that corporate fascism is downtown's *nom de guerre*, well, just so long's the checks don't bounce, ja? We've a mountain to raise thru it all, don't y'know, & by the stars & the skidmarks on dead Gurdjieff's lost britches we will do so.

It's all a big circle an old potato-head poet once said, that y'do just as much evil in this life as good... that ol' poet knew 'bout cycles of intention, yeah he did, but when art's tang befalleth Main Street, well now ain't that just a hoot & a grace, girl... ?

SHARK DRAG

what're sharks is this very thing we
try to do's the evaporate of how odd
how utterly collaborative that said
quick collaging for ear is instantly
the one-handed barmaid only one
hereabouts e'er seen before & no
way to tell her the one full breast's
palpably heavier than the other this
very contingency & field expedience
of such costumes such intricate hang
time nor actual side not heavier than
each fully knowing & telling in every
fashion full breadth'd flimflamfilmy
fingered on yr echo resonatedly each

*

SPLASH RESEARCH

we the mind tonguéd gape soundmusteredly
we are frankly looking without blink at all
seaworthy & suspense rapt as depth or rapt
as breadth or ever sea speakéd that very
foolful rapacidity rapidly reaping so raving
is fingered thru is abandoned now this
perfect season its splash research there
wherever & everlasting squid whippery &
how can we not try to save one another &
why is undigested Tatum & the eating of
glass the very essence of the very overbite
that is Toledo's echo down along the Ohio
& yes we are a long way from any coast save
the many minded sounding & rogue'd withal

**

In The Theatre Of Perfect Speed . . .

Until my mountain breaks the surface of the waters, call my mountain seamount, know my mountain teems with oddest lovelies invisible to man. That ocean-knowing predators still cruise the subaqua, that the subaqua is both medium and solution, till the time.

Seamount reeks of gimcrack, jerrybuild, and Desire. And the greatest of these goes without saying, without the impulse to confession, explication, or Define. For there are Shadows on the Mount, and the subaqua wavers densely, indubitably, with Defiles in Suspension, awaiting my Direction.

In this Dim the mustered defiles behold one another and are not alone, are not without the pure pose, lit just so and miked withal, the whole scripted, molded, shaped, and timed to the merest eel, weed, and Reel. We are in the theatre of light, the theatre of perfect speed, and we will not blink.

Captain of my mountain's rising, Carpenter of the shingless ceiling come unhinged, Caroler of dolor and dismay revised, Christa the Makar nigh unto lamentation laminated, till Time itself is jigsawed piecework spun and plighted seamlessly in all dreamt and redreamt savor and stun, striven for and won.

I have loitered in the rye, gaped upon the moving figures who serve tipplers sans the tip. I, too, have leered, howsoever coyly, covertly, complicitously vulnerable and yet hungry to rip the cover from the lie. My ruined lungs hold breaths too knowing, full knowing I will rise and break the surface.

Will I? Could I? Did I? Do I? This terrible
swimming Toward... into grottos beneath
the waves, guileful hardly less than gullible;
trusting, trysting, testy, terrified, and tough.

What is this terrible romance

with Light?

Can the collaboratives even exist

uncontesting?

Who am I to scam my own

submergency?

Full knowing I will rise can be no more than
boasting, and boasting is one fault I can no
longer afford. The time of rising, of leveraged
liquidity ladled aloud, visible as the sun's own
broad tomahawk, has come to claim its wound.

*

STAMPEDIMENTA

sometimes a wound howsoever inadvertent is
simply too great a shark's wide-eyed bite &
stampeded school sapped in the midst is &
this is admitted on the cusp of the successive
it's the when you know you know syndrome
as tidal flux frisked doublebind criss & crux
as has been heard &'s being that bite you bet
they a moving testament unable to cease the
savor all planktonic & bashboard chRomantic
& yea tho' we float so rarely these days are
uncomma'd enjamb'd thar she boweth above
the common sinks with curses & lust curdle
all asplash on most sides as they come/goeth
mouthing lager as seawater lest they drown

***

DOLLY PARTING

because Jack's not only Jack Jack's also
the music which is no mean mouthful no
despairing Other nor not immediate & on
going Jack's the net escaped which is this
music too & how many get to know that let
alone honor that or & how's this for unsung
begot to participate in that briefest of everly
lasted glimpses sounded in the famous midst
o! raucous chest thumpery slipped as some
nooses chaos dodged this time even if only
this very time & all those seas of inattention
seizures of leakage that very liquidity upon
a dolly parting the Red Sea of Quid Quo
proferred but mustneeds deferred indeed

****

Listening Post Tempo Breath . . .

The bell's a drum's an assemblage on a page's how time's panic
wreaks resonance. And what's *that* if not the makings of, the
splicings of, the very tappings and the cuttings of, that which
is a horror and an exhaltation in these, the summer eves of
mountains rising, others subsiding, and whatever fadeth?

My bell drops slowly into attenuating echo, sounds fishtailing,
brooded on by wakes and currents both intemperate and wry.
My bell swings amidst the all too busy competings of this, the
subaqua. At the portals, isolate and apparent as a fattened
slug upon a pane, my silhouette: doth the poet yet breathe?

Three congas, high tones down to deep tones and all the wee
tricky hand moves to modulate the in betweens; patterns and
the violation of patterns comprising all guileful descents alike
the weaves and ascents and interruptus, too; lost below seas
where shards catch glimpsings but are themselves unseen.

Let glued splicings of midnight's cuttings in glossy periodicals
warp and buckle and melt amidst subaqua's dilutionary hove.
Each sparkled glance undone, each unfixed echo slid awry,
for the oceanic has no blink upon this globe's whole 'round,
nor do grief or grievance stay fastened 'neath these swells.

For the Midwest is a listening post unclocked, but yea thee
are being watched on here, and seizures ease disciplined goals,
too: The mount's a bell's a drum's an assemblage on a page's
how each tympanum cocks and nods, how the vastly spirited
lap at spigots no more phallic than forests lapping Time itself.

Shall I? Would I? Can I? Am I? I've beaten
back traces of despair (and well we've mixed...
we're the band plays the storefront on Vine;
front door open; madmen y'all come, since '96!)

What other yearnings save

sound pursued & mixt?

Can these collaged racings persist

a city angels flee?

Who am I to riff these others'

ears, dues, & duende, too?

This unclocked tempo breath of drumpo' song
unwitnessed, nor volunteered, yet volunteers...
in diving bells of our own devising, devised on
the improvised instant... transpontaneously
dug in, our fulcrum these Plains mute panic.

*

LIQUIDITY LAGER

who gets what image & what's cut is her
lower lip & its hang askew above all that
cannot be aligned save in this lager of
laboring its together'd liquidity & how
ear's access to oceanic rogue foolery fully
meant yet unspoke her voice totalled in
futility & girlish & despondent plea that
we togetherers cock to is the very labor
of myriad quick cutting uninterruptedly
a liquidity so fluent so instantaneously
chopworthy there that very image of
suspended with all uneven & bit lipped
above that which does not match yet
which sway balances mind tonguédly

*****

PURCHASE GUARANTEED

willful & obstinate incontinence never meant
not forgetful rogue drollery surge surfed upon
those widest of wide open shark bait besotted
icicle bicycle tentacle seasons swum off from
& this is that part about poise self possession
the part about no guarantees & always alert
to 'cause swum off from's another only modus
another only Way to swim with whatever
else's Out There not just the sharks neither
blink nor stop casing the sea the way thieves
case it's why sharks're criminals I suppose at
least insofar as are that when they presume
to purchase as opposed to take bites out of
which is what they really do sharks buy-bye

******

Things A Body To Its Detriment Gets Used To . . .

Am the para-Michael, flesh-bound witness-cum-diarist, the guerilla brother in middle-aged whiteman drag lurking filmonic yet extra-performative interstices, poetry's faux daemon in leaky shoes & my father's silver timepiece.

What is so very unexpected in the attempt to do poetry is how this is an activity that makes out of what the doer is, in the sense that the poet defines a *locus definitiva*, wherein the forces of poetry locate, solely.

The attempt is to speak of a cyclic & self-fulfilling feed-off. Things a body to its detriment gets used to. This is about *routes*, & how routes are indispensible & route fabrication takes research. In a bar, for instance, the contract's simple: a pretty woman asks you if you want another. That a bar's a form of show business needs only be said once. The bartender, conversely, must be prepared to ask that question repeatedly, thru the night: want another? To its detriment, the body replies in the affirmative, also repeatedly, be that body male or female. The pretty woman, too, is either male or female, & the 'notherliness goes on & on, at the trough prophetically... what is self-fulfilling fathers Time itself, that *locus definitiva*, the sound of surprise, the arc of azimuthal hallelujah, in deep & dancing... indepenDance.

Or one I saw recently, said she had a cracked windshield... you just knew, at least in her case, she'd fallen in love with the play of light along the fault line. Never would, I'd guess, get that windshield fixed. Just to've *found* this barmaid took the most diligent research! & research will be our topic from now on... not only how to do research, but why do it, and *where*.

Para-Michael's route extends telephonically, postal-officiously, thru the town's taverns, across its jittery & untrustworthy streets, from ill to yea. Whate'er that route, to follow it where it wends mustneeds be *this* occupation, this *poetique*.

How situate at the locus?

The doer is a physical being, near as we can tell. Poetry is a made, bar none, and its plane of making is the body; where poetry wends is sinewy, bloody, hairy, pulsing, stumbly & leapish, fully contingent on gravity and coordination, spatial resonance and actual echo, wet atmosphere as it were, lungs, the eyes blinking, the bowels roiling, a steadied hand, balance & sway, the sore lip & the arthritic joint, that which has been abused & that which wears out, the calls to intimacy, love's very own yearn, thwart, cry, cringe, & watchfulness, cocked.

As the body's timebound, so too the poem pulses forth. And to each part of the poem, its exaltation & decay: to find the point to set the poem free of the body, the release point, the saying point, its telling. We do this work so that this work, released, tells back upon us, spelling our sentence, timing our destinies. We go tell it on the mountains raised. If we can raise them. We circle our rising mountains in wet air resonatedly, enginous wording the band at full capacity, steamed & percussive. There! One-five-two manned, by volunteers... *Volunteers*! No one asked permission, yet permission is given. No one commanded a film be concocted... the film, quite the same as the poem, is volunteered. Even our cinemanuensis volunteers.

We research the *locus definitiva* where our feet meet earth's arc precisely. Precisely touching. Pretending, *precisely* . . .

Specifica y Conclusivitas . . .

PRE-TENSE: the Azimuthal Hallelujah
Surface-of-Consciousness: PAN-ACTUAL
locus definitiva: the subaqua

MU-PSYCHE: Rhythming Spontane Improv
Obtrusions-*du-Jour*:   STARS & SKIDMARKS
notable proviso: to mock and mime them

MODAL OPERANDI: Steam thru Time
Unasked-for-Permissions: GIVEN
the directive: to circle on the rise

Strapped in upon the goggle nearby, asquint & without that manner of mercy defiant of a body's detriment, 14th Street floats in August: techne & optics & the wracking manipulations of impure stock laid in as this summer's neglected doorway's cycles of intention, as survivabilities along bright fault lines & as celluloidal liquiditas from now on & on out, long as it takes.

An autopsy will be performed, according to visional specs of our own devising. Yea, & Humpty will be reassembled, the lie of the Egg Man's deconstruction will be uncovered. Many-minded me grandfathers mine own. I'm all. I'm it. Nothing's changed.

This is indeed where collaboration runs off the track. The contributors have co-operated and are dismissed. The scam's grum chaos is levered incrementally, spun with intricate torpidity upward, its facets coming unglued, warping & buckling & minutely re-availed. The one with the bags under her eyes? She's the One. Hers is the only submergency suborned.

You thought this would be a quickie maybe, yeah? You thought yr favorite bits & tics might weather the slice & dice unscathed maybe, just mayhaps? On into September's drool cellblockaded is closer to the mark, the mark being what you have made of yourself... quick now & once again: the pressure is on, utterly, quite as it has ever been, oyez.

It ain't a movie till it's a movie. Bust yr guts tho' ye will, the glassy surface covers all yr bets. Cover yr ass as ye will, you ain't fit company namore, not till the time. The time is nigh. Has e'er & will e'er.

The thing about the blues is irrepressibility, yet it is that very quality that's kept sleighted from view. The monks & every Newport dancer share in this: the rhythm of the cheese, too, touches precisely.

We have come to the posture arena's pick & choose pain in the lower back & migraines. Can our mountain be made to fly, did we take & retake sans saki quite enough? Did our impurifying of the stock give us this day?

O! we're winging it now. By the wind from our tails we sail forth, bright-eyed cutters all. Thar she boweth, Ahab's leer, Tenzing's triumph: *your* way!

THE VISIONAL, *EN PASSANT*

in the beginning the Lord sayeth
be all Eye,
as the Spirited Seas are, utterly
which also have I made
sayeth the Lord

thus was it so from long ago
that there were *Voyeurs*, oyez
and so it came to pass
that *Voyeurs* found myriad motes
as dire dastard in all panoramas
& further that the Seas themselves
teemed with prey of every manner

& that lastly the Lord sayeth
let there be Poets to roust & swim
with all dire dastard in *Voyeurs'* eyes
& as for those very Seas' every prey
directives will be forthcoming
sayeth the Lord

nota bene: CAUSATIVA

In the Fall of 1995, I was in the waning weeks of temporary tenure with **THE LAST BOPPERS**, a Cincinnati-based jazz ensemble, serving as poet and percussionist. Also that season, first-time filmmaker Aralee Strange was mounting a stage production derived from the script of her budding film, **THIS TRAIN,** an independent project for which she hoped her stage adaptation would provide publicity & future funding prospects.

One intriguing aspect of both her film & its staged extract was to be her use of selected Ohio poets, delivering their work in a cafe setting, somewhat in the manner of the classic open poetry reading, uncensored and wholly solipse. The basic template for the staged cafe readings would be derived from the kinds of poetry shenanigans then occuring under the hosting aegis of Ken Kawaji, a poet serving at that time as the poetry organizer at **KALDI'S**, a multi-ambitioned bookstore/bar/caberet/coffeehouse/cafe/playroom on Main Street in Cincinnati's gritty downtown neighborhood, Over-the-Rhine.

My own contribution to the staged project was to assemble a jazz/poetry trio which, besides providing our particular mix of urban-based jazz & poetry, also functioned as a performance resource for the other poets, and as ambience backdrop for the staging as a whole. Our trio found no place for itself in the eventual filming two and a half years later, but we of the jazz/poetry ilk have continued to do that performative thing we do, and have also continued, in spirit at least, to honor the inclusion of performer poets in the film itself.

Hail to these, my trio-mates, Jack Walker & Ken Leslie: to their ears, chops, & soul, yea, this writ of *habeus corpus poetique* is also heartily dedicated . . .

-r's e
(cinci/july '98)

el oddmenta poemas:

SHARK DRAG --- the one-handed barmaid works
        on Madison, in Covington, a joint called
        THE PAD, name's Laura.

SPLASH RESEARCH --- many good poets travel
        down to the Ohio River from Toledo; they
        stay with Brian & Dawn & are rather loud.

STAMPEDIMENTA --- it was the Kent Ohio poet
        Doug Baird who claimed you didn't have
        to break a board over his head; the poets of
        Kent were said to be notorious drunkards.

DOLLY PARTING --- braggarts & back scratchers
        make dubious mentors, rather in the same
        manner inattentive audiences make piss
        poor poets & even worse musicians.

LIQUIDITY LAGER --- chops are to musicians
        what editing is to auteurs: keep the razor's
        edge nigh on where the sun don't shine.

PURCHASE GUARANTEED --- it's the dead, it's
        the dead, it's the dead & all their dollar bills
        who rule this world ... shark bait beware.

The definition below descends to these barrens courtesy of
THE EVOKED & EMBODIED STANDARD DICTIONARY
OF BUDDHA BALONEY & OTHER ASSORTED & ARCANE
MYTHOS-ILLOGICAL IMPROV . . .

cin-e-ma-nu-en-sing / accented 5th syllable; spoken in a rapid flow; (comb. *cinema-amanuensis-sing*; the 2d comp., **amanuensis**, freq. meant 'literary secretary,' i.e. *"Young Ezra found employment as William Butler Yeats' amanuensis, learning thereby certain wiles to sing as poets sing, prior to their becoming cinematic."* That poets have, in these the latter days, taken up the craft of rendering motion pictures, thereby becoming cinematic indeed, gives rise to the new terminology.) **1** : a voluntary activity wherein a third party, typically poet, secretarily bears witness to other poets' handling of the spirits of poetry whilst they are engaging in the rendering of motion picture art **a** : those poetry-type scribblings onesuch third party might do tangential to secretarily bearing said witness **b** : saidsame scribblings, published as text and distributed as book **2** : an orality of poet sentiment involuntarily sounded aloud by a third party, another poet usually, whilst secretarily engaged by attendance to yet other poets' manipulat'g of *l'esprit de poesis* whilst fabricat'g like cinematographic renderings **a** : the published transcriptions of saidsuch resoundings **3** : what you're holding in your hand, as if you didn't know what a writ of *habeus corpus poetique* is . . .

ARALEE STRANGE

Prior to moving to Cincinnati, Aralee Strange, a native of Birmingham Alabama, lived and worked in Atlanta GA, Cambridge MA, and New York NY. Beginning in 1987, in collaboration with fellow Cincinnati poet Jim Palmarini, Strange began and conducted several open poetry reading series and read regularly at a host of regional venues.

I first encountered her participating in the late '80s at the April Aegis Poetry Festival, Bill Polak's annual multi-day, multi-venue all-open poetry festival in Kent, Ohio. She was a poet/playwright whose body of work included *Etta Stone: A Film for Radio* (1990), which she wrote, produced and edited @ WGUC, Cincinnati (aired nationally on NPR stations, included in WGBH's Arts&Ideas series); *dr. pain on main* (1991), a play based on her series of poems by the same name, commissioned and produced by Cincinnati Playhouse in the Park; *The Chronicles of Plague* (1992), commissioned and produced by Ensemble Theatre of Cincinnati; *An Evening at the Sad Cafe* (1995), a series of directed scenes from her screenplay, *This Train*, performed at Ensemble Theatre of Cincinnati & Carnegie Arts Center (1997). *This Train* (production begun late '90s, ended filming 2001), the feature film she wrote, directed & edited, was still in post-production at the time of her death.

Aralee moved from Ohio to Athens, GA in March 2007, where she initiated the much celebrated *Word of Mouth* feature/open poetry series at the Globe on the first Wednesday of each month, which series continues to this day.

ABOUT THE AUTHOR

RALPH LA CHARITY

With compañero poets Ken Kawaji and Bill Polak, La Charity created the two hour weekly jazz/poetry broadcast, the *Skaldric Cauldron*, on WAIF/FM radio Cincinnati in the mid-'90s. Working as poet/percussionist with Cincinnati jazzmen Ricardo Williams and Jack Walker, he created the village jazz cohort, *SàSemblé*, a poetry and music crew that appeared at various venues in Ohio and Pennsylvania from 1996 thru 2001, including at different times poets and musicians James Quilligan, Scott Hisey, Anne Marie La Charity, Brian Richards, Bill Polak, and Steve Lansky. His poetics samizdat, *W'ORCs/ALOUD ALLOWED*, began publishing from Amsterdam, Holland in 1986, and continued its run through West Germany, San Antonio, and Cincinnati, having published to date over 90 issues.

At http://www.semantikon.com/dialect.htm, selected compendia of his work are available, archived for the years 2005 and 2008 by sitemaster Lance Oditt.

At www.athenswordofmouth.com, individual pieces of his were posted by Aralee Strange, from the years 2010 thru 2013. He currently appears delivering his poetry aloud as an open participant at open poetry readings throughout the State of Ohio.

Books by Dos Madres Press

Mary Margaret Alvarado - *Hey Folly* (2013)
John Anson - *Jose-Maria de Heredia's Les Trophées* (2013)
Jennifer Arin - *Ways We Hold* (2012)
Michael Autrey - *From The Genre Of Silence* (2008)
Paul Bray - *Things Past and Things to Come* (2006), *Terrible Woods* (2008)
Jon Curley - *New Shadows* (2009), *Angles of Incidents* (2012)
Sara Dailey - *Earlier Lives* (2012)
Richard Darabaner - *Plaint* (2012)
Deborah Diemont - *Wanderer* (2009), *Diverting Angels* (2012)
Joseph Donahue - *The Copper Scroll* (2007)
Annie Finch - *Home Birth* (2004)
Norman Finkelstein - *An Assembly* (2004), *Scribe* (2009)
Gerry Grubbs - *Still Life* (2005), *Girls in Bright Dresses Dancing* (2010),
    The Hive-a book we read for its honey (2013)
Ruth D. Handel - *Tugboat Warrior* (2013)
Richard Hague - *Burst, Poems Quickly* (2004),
    During The Recent Extinctions (2012)
Pauletta Hansel - *First Person* (2007), *What I Did There* (2011)
Michael Heller - *A Look at the Door with the Hinges Off* (2006),
    Earth and Cave (2006)
Michael Henson - *The Tao of Longing & The Body Geographic* (2010)
R. Nemo Hill - *When Men Bow Down* (2012)
W. Nick Hill - *And We'd Understand Crows Laughing* (2012)
Eric Hoffman - *Life At Braintree* (2008), *The American Eye* (2011),
    By The Hours (2013)
James Hogan - *Rue St. Jacques* (2005)
Keith Holyoak - *My Minotaur* (2010), *Foreigner* (2012)
Nancy Kassell - *Text(isles)* (2013)
David M. Katz - *Claims of Home* (2011)
Sherry Kearns - *Deep Kiss* (2013)
Burt Kimmelman - *There Are Words* (2007), *The Way We Live* (2011)
Pamela L. Laskin - *Plagiarist* (2012)
Owen Lewis - *Sometimes Full of Daylight* (2013)
Richard Luftig - *Off The Map* (2006)
Austin MacRae - *The Organ Builder* (2012)

Mario Markus - *Chemical Poems-One For Each Element* (2013)
J. Morris - *The Musician, Approaching Sleep* (2006)
Rick Mullin - *Soutine* (2012), *Coelacanth* (2013)
Robert Murphy - *Not For You Alone* (2004), *Life in the Ordovician* (2007),
　　From Behind The Blind (2013)
Pam O'Brien - *The Answer To Each Is The Same* (2012)
Peter O'Leary - *A Mystical Theology of the Limbic Fissure* (2005)
Bea Opengart - *In The Land* (2011)
David A. Petreman - *Candlelight in Quintero - bilingual edition* (2011)
Paul Pines - *Reflections in a Smoking Mirror* (2011), *New Orleans Variations
　　& Paris Ouroboros* (2013)
David Schloss - *Behind the Eyes* (2005)
William Schickel - *What A Woman* (2007)
Lianne Spidel & Anne Loveland - *Pairings* (2012)
Murray Shugars - *Songs My Mother Never Taught Me* (2011),
　　Snakebit Kudzu (2013)
Jason Shulman - *What does reward bring you but to bind you to Heaven
　　like a slave? (2013)*
Olivia Stiffler - *Otherwise, we are safe* (2013)
Carole Stone - *Hurt, the Shadow- the Josephine Hopper poems* (2013)
Nathan Swartzendruber - *Opaque Projectionist* (2009)
Jean Syed - *Sonnets* (2009)
Madeline Tiger - *The Atheist's Prayer* (2010), *From the Viewing Stand* (2011)
James Tolan - *Red Walls* (2011)
Brian Volck - *Flesh Becomes Word* (2013)
Henry Weinfield - *The Tears of the Muses* (2005),
　　Without Mythologies (2008), *A Wandering Aramaean* (2012)
Donald Wellman - *A North Atlantic Wall* (2010),
　　The Cranberry Island Series (2012)
Anne Whitehouse - *The Refrain* (2012)
Martin Willetts Jr. - *Secrets No One Must Talk About* (2011)
Tyrone Williams - *Futures, Elections* (2004), *Adventures of Pi* (2011)
Kip Zegers - *The Poet of Schools* (2013)

www.dosmadres.com

Printed by Libri Plureos GmbH in Hamburg, Germany